REBEL GIRLS

Little Library

10 Women who Play Sports

This is a work of creative nonfiction. It is a collection of heartwarming and thought-provoking stories inspired by the lives and adventures of influential women. It is not an encyclopedic account of the events and accomplishments of their lives.

www.rebelgirls.com

Rebel Girls, Inc.
421 Elm Ave.
Larkspur, CA 94939

Text by Dinah Dunn
Art direction by Giulia Flamini
Graphic design by Kristen Brittain
Graphic design and additional illustrations: Alessandro Raimondo
Portrait illustrations: 4: Luisa Rivera, 8: Lucy Nightingale,
12: Emmanuelle Walker, 16: Maya McKibbin, 20: Kim Holt,
24: Lily Kim Qian, 28: Camilla Ru, 32: Eline Van Dam,
36: Kate Prior, 40: Deandra Hodge

Printed in China, 2023
10 9 8 7 6 5 4 3 2 1
ISBN: 979-8-88964-073-8

FSC
www.fsc.org
MIX
Paper | Supporting responsible forestry
FSC™ C018179

CONTENTS

Anne Wafula Strike

Wheelchair Racer

Born May 8, 1969 | Kenya and UK

One day in Kenya, a two-year-old girl named Anne became very, very sick. Her parents were worried. They took her to a hospital. The doctors said she had a disease called polio. Eventually, Anne got better. But she could no longer walk.

Many people in Anne's village did not understand what polio was. The local healer said evil magic made it so she could not walk. Her neighbors called her a snake because she had to crawl to get around.

Her body worked differently now, but Anne kept moving. She learned to use crutches. Then she got a wheelchair. Her father found a school that taught children with disabilities. Anne did well in school. She became the first person in her family to go to college.

When Anne grew up, she became a teacher. She fell in love with another teacher named Norman. Norman was from Essex, England. They decided to get married and move there together.

One day, Anne went to the local running track to exercise. She circled around it in her wheelchair. A coach noticed her. *Have you ever tried racing?* the coach asked. Anne hadn't! But she was excited to try.

It turned out that Anne was fast—very fast. Two years later,

Anne competed in the Paralympic Games. The Paralympics are just like the Olympics, but for athletes with disabilities. Anne was the first wheelchair racer from Africa to compete there.

In 2006, Anne became a British citizen. The next year, she won a bronze medal at the Paralympic World Cup. The crowd clapped and cheered as she competed for her new home—Great Britain.

SCAN TO HEAR MORE!

Benedetta Pilato

Swimmer

Born January 18, 2005 | Italy

Benedetta's heart pounded as she entered the pool area. The 16-year-old swimmer had already won medals for her breaststroke, but she was nervous. Today, she was competing against some of the best swimmers in Europe.

Benedetta took off her black sweatshirt. She pulled on her goggles. Then she climbed onto the starting block. She felt her energy build as she waited for the race to start. *BUZZZZ!* The buzzer sounded and the race began.

Benedetta dove in and came up halfway across the pool. Her strong arms pushed through the water. She quickly pulled ahead of the other swimmers. She was in the lead!

Taking deep breaths, she pushed herself harder. She couldn't see the other swimmers. She was racing against herself. And Benedetta knew she was swimming well. Would she break the European record?

When she reached the end of the lane, Benedetta touched the edge of the pool. The whole arena started cheering. Her Italian fans clapped the loudest.

Benedetta took off her swim cap and laughed. The time on the board said 29.30 seconds. She hadn't just broken the European record—she had broken the world record for the 50-meter breaststroke!

Benedetta couldn't believe it. "Oh, I'm really happy," she said. "I didn't think I could make this now. I thought I might break the European record but definitely not the world record." She had been winning medals since she was 14. But for this minute, she was the fastest swimmer in the world!

Tennis Player

Born November 22, 1943 | USA

Billie Jean King played tennis for the first time in fifth grade. With a racket in her hand, she knew that she had found her sport. She liked the speed. She liked the *POP* when she hit the ball hard. But most of all, she liked winning.

Billie Jean told her mom, "I'm going to be number one in the world." She practiced whenever she could. Soon she was taking home trophies from tournaments.

In 1966, Billie Jean won her first Wimbledon, one of the biggest tennis tournaments in the world. She was so proud of herself! But her prize money was less than half of what the men's winner got.

Win after win, Billie was soon ranked number one in the world. But each time, she earned less than male champions did. It wasn't fair!

Instead of being angry, Billie Jean decided to fix it. She helped create the Women's Tennis Association. As its first president, she worked to make tournaments pay the same for men and women.

Some people weren't happy with her push for equality on the court. Bobby Riggs was one of those people. He had once been the number one men's player. He challenged Billie to a match. He was sure he could beat her.

Billie agreed. "I love to win," she said. "Bobby had better be ready!" But inside, she was afraid. What if she lost? People might think men were better players than women.

With 90 million people watching, Billie beat Bobby in three matches in a row. She won $100,000 and the admiration of tennis fans worldwide.

Billie Jean won many more tournaments, including a record 20 Wimbledons. But she will be remembered for her role in making women's sports both exciting and equal.

SCAN TO HEAR MORE!

Brigette Lacquette

Ice Hockey Player

Born November 10, 1992 | Canada

At five years old, Brigette couldn't wait to lace up her skates. Her dad had flooded the yard and let it freeze. Now she and her sister and brother could play hockey every day!

Brigette's tiny First Nations town of Mallard, Manitoba, in Canada didn't have a rink. There were only 120 people!

Its size was a problem when Brigette wanted to join a hockey team. While there were teams for boys closer to her home, there weren't many for girls. But her family knew how much the game meant to Brigette. They found her a team and drove hours to get her to practices and games.

Brigette shone on the ice. She was thrilled to be playing the game she loved. But it was hard to leave her small town. She was usually the only First Nations player on the team.

When she played her first big tournament at 12 years old, she heard words that stung. Girls on the other teams called her nasty names. Why were they so mean? Her father told her not to worry about them. “Beat them on the ice,” he said.

Brigette took her father’s advice. She wasn’t going to let them stop her. Instead, she worked on her slapshot. She became great at defense. She played in college and then professionally.

In 2018, she made Canada's Olympic hockey team! She also made history. She was the only First Nations woman who had ever made the team. She couldn't wait to tell her dad the news. She called him up, laughing and crying.

"Congratulations, my girl," he said. He was crying as well. "You definitely earned it."

Megan Rapinoe

Soccer Player

Born July 5, 1985 | USA

Megan and the United States women's soccer team had won the World Cup in 2015. So they knew they had a chance to win again in 2019. But they were playing against some great teams.

The first game against Thailand proved they could. They beat Thailand 13–0. They scored the most goals ever in a single World Cup game. Megan scored again when they beat Chile, 3–0, and Spain, 2–1. They were on their way!

But Megan was nervous about the next game against France. They were the toughest team the United States had faced.

The pressure was on for another reason. Before the game, Megan took a stand. Usually, winning teams visit with their government leaders. But she felt President Trump didn't fight for the same things she did, such as equal rights for everyone. So she said that if the team won the World Cup, she wouldn't go to the White House. President Trump got angry and said she'd have to win first. Now, the whole world was watching to see if she did.

Five minutes into the game, Megan scored the first goal. She raised her arms and smiled at the crowd. *We will not back down!* she thought. She scored again in the second half. The team won that game, 2–1, but Megan had hurt her leg. She couldn't play during the team's next game against England. Would she play in the finals against the Netherlands?

Not only did she play, but she also scored the first of two goals that won the team the World Cup! She was named player and best scorer of the tournament. Megan stayed true to her beliefs and didn't visit the White House. But she and the team celebrated with a huge parade in New York City.

SCAN TO HEAR MORE!

Figure Skater

Born July 7, 1980 | USA

Even as a young girl, Michelle was something special on the ice. Like her older brother and sister, she loved to skate. And she was good at it. At six years old, she won the first competition she entered.

That's when Michelle's parents decided they would do whatever it took to help her succeed. There wasn't a lot of money for fancy costumes or new skates. So her mom borrowed costumes and bought used skates. Michelle's dad woke up in the dark to drive her to skating practice.

One day, she was messing around on the ice and her father got upset. He said, "I pay a lot of money to have these lessons. Don't waste my time.

Don't waste Coach's time. Don't waste your time."

Her dad's words stuck with her. She never wasted another moment. When she was 11 years old, she and her sister Karen started training with a famous coach. The next year, she was competing at the US Figure Skating Championships. She came in sixth place! A few years later, she won her first of five world championships.

Michelle set her eyes on the 1998 Olympics in Japan. Tears came to her eyes when she skated in the Olympic arena. She couldn't see them, but she knew her parents were watching. She had dreamed of this moment since she was seven years old. She had finally made it!

The competition came down to Michelle and another American skater, Tara Lipinski. Michelle's beautiful routine earned good marks from the judges.

But there was a small chance that Tara could beat her. Michelle's heart sank as she watched Tara skate her best. Tara's marks were higher.

Michelle was proud that she had reached her dream. And she was quick to remind her fans: "I didn't lose the gold. I won the silver."

Tennis Player

Born September 26, 1981 | USA

Before Serena was born, her dad knew she would play tennis. He had taught himself to play. He thought she could make money playing professionally. But he could not imagine how far Serena would go!

Serena began playing when she was four years old. She and her sisters would go to the court every chance they could. They worked hard on their shots and their swings.

At the time, there weren't many Black girls playing tennis. Her dad knew they would not always be treated well at competitions. So he asked kids to boo the girls while they played. It was embarrassing! But it helped Serena learn not to listen to what other people said. It was the most important lesson of her life.

Serena and her older sister Venus both became very good. Her dad thought they could be the top two tennis players in the world. So she started to work toward that goal.

When she was 14, Serena started winning titles and trophies. Sometimes she played doubles with Venus. Sometimes the sisters played against each other in a match.

Venus pushed Serena. "It was difficult for me to play Venus because she'd always beat me so badly," Serena said. She had to train harder just to compete with her sister.

All of that pushing helped make Serena one of the greatest tennis players of all time. She won four gold medals at the Olympics and 39 Grand Slam titles. And her dad was right: she could make money playing tennis. She has earned more than any other woman in sports history.

In 2022, Serena said she might stop playing in tournaments. She has a lot of other things she wants to learn, such as acting and designing clothes. And if Serena wants something, she will work until she gets it.

SCAN TO HEAR MORE!

Simone Biles

Gymnast

Born March 14, 1997 | USA

Once there was a girl named Simone who grew up with her grandparents in Texas. She had a lot of energy. She loved to run and jump on the trampoline.

When she was six years old, she visited a gym. She could not believe what she was seeing! Girls were flipping through the air. They were leaping on the balance beam. They were rolling across the floor. Simone wanted to try!

She was so good that the coach sent a letter to her grandparents. Could Simone come back and train? Soon, she was flipping and rolling like the girls she'd seen. Simone was the smallest kid in the gym. But she quickly became one of the best.

When she was 14, Simone won her first national competition. No one could take their eyes off her amazing moves. Two years later, she was the first Black girl to win a gold medal in the World Championships! By the end of 2020, Simone had earned five Olympic medals and 25 world championship medals.

Everyone thought Simone would win a gold medal at the Tokyo Olympics. But when she was there, she didn't feel right. It felt scary when she was in the air. She didn't want to let down her team. But she might hurt herself if she competed.

She said, "I learned that it's okay not to be okay." So Simone sat out most of the competition in Tokyo. But she was always ready to cheer on her team.

Simone has the most medals in the history of gymnastics. She even has four moves named after her! That's why she is known as the "GOAT," or **G**reatest **o**f **A**ll **T**ime.

SCAN TO HEAR MORE!

Sky Brown

Skateboarder

Born July 7, 2008 | Japan and UK

Sky loved to watch her dad skateboard. He could zoom up a half-pipe and do tricks. “I just thought, ‘I want to do that,’ so I did,” she said.

She started by balancing on her dad’s board. At first, he was afraid she would fall and hurt herself. She was so young! But soon she was so good he bought her a board.

When Sky went to the skate park to practice, boys would sometimes cut in front of her. It made Sky mad. It also pushed her to be better. “As I got older,” she said, “I just wanted to show the boys what’s up.”

Sky trained harder and jumped higher. She learned new tricks by watching YouTube videos. When she was 10 years old, she became the youngest professional skater ever!

Nobody gets good at skating without some bloody knees and elbows. Sky has fallen off her board many times. Once, when she was trying a trick on a half-pipe, she fell and broke a bunch of bones. She had to be flown to the hospital. But once she got better, she went right back to skating.

When Sky was 12, she became the youngest person in British history to go to the Olympics. She was excited to go. “I knew people from all around the world would be watching,” she said. “Even if just one little girl watches, I wanted to inspire her.”

During her first two runs, Sky fell. But on the third try, she won a bronze medal for her skating.

Skateboarding is not the only thing Sky does well. She surfs professionally too. Plus she likes to dance. She was on the TV show *Dancing with the Stars: Juniors*. She won that too! Is there anything Sky can’t do?

Para Dressage Rider

Born March 13, 2001 | UK

Once upon a time, there was a girl named Tegan who just wanted to do what other kids could do. She was born with quadriplegic cerebral palsy. This means her body can get as stiff as a tree. It can be hard for her to move her arms and legs. Sometimes her muscles shake, and it is difficult to talk.

When Tegan was five years old, her parents took her to a horse-riding school near their home in Bristol, England. It had classes for people with disabilities. Tegan felt right at home there.

She felt free when she was riding. What started as fun soon became so much more. Soon, she was riding all the time.

One day, Tegan watched riders compete in the Paralympics. She decided she wanted to compete too! She chose a sport called dressage. Tegan describes it as "ballet on a horse."

Dressage works only if the horse and rider trust each other. Tegan guides her horse through moves. When they work well together, they flow like a dance. She has won many titles already.

Tegan wants to be the first Black British woman to go to the Paralympics for horseback riding. "I want people of all shapes and sizes to be able to join the sport," she said.

When Tegan is not practicing dressage, she makes fun videos on

TikTok. She talks about her life and what it's like to live with cerebral palsy. The story of her goal to get to the Paralympics was also made into a movie. She hopes her story inspires others to dream big.

About Rebel Girls

Rebel Girls is a global, multi-platform empowerment brand dedicated to helping raise the most inspired and confident generation of girls through content, experiences, products, and community. Originating from an international best-selling children's book, Rebel Girls amplifies stories of real-life women throughout history, geography, and field of excellence. With a growing community of nearly 20 million self-identified Rebel Girls spanning more than 100 countries, the brand engages with Generation Alpha through its book series, award-winning podcast, events, and merchandise. With the 2021 launch of the Rebel Girls app, the company has created a flagship destination for girls to explore a wondrous world filled with inspiring true stories of extraordinary women.

As a B Corp, we're part of a global community of businesses that meet high standards of social and environmental impact.

Join the Rebel Girls community:

Facebook: facebook.com/rebelgirls
Instagram: @rebelgirls
Twitter: @rebelgirlsbook
TikTok: @rebelgirlsbook
Web: rebelgirls.com
Podcast: rebelgirls.com/podcast
App: rebelgirls.com/audio

If you liked this book, please take a moment to review it wherever you prefer!